Sunrise Sunset

Sunrise Sunset

B. Jacquelyn Smith

To the Family of Humankind

Sunrise/Sunset

Creative energies evolved a fresh new niche over time
using land and water resources.
This space that they inhabit is known as a marsh,
covered part of the year with standing water.
These wetlands give us free services: flood
control,
natural filtration,
prevention of saltwater intruding inland,
habitats to eat, spawn, stopover, raise offspring,
and recreation for us.
In order to continue to enjoy the wetlands and its wildlife,
we must not take more than our share
building structures,
cultivate only native species,
be conscious of fertilizer use,
and maintain our own population at a balanced level.
Then the graceful Great Blue Heron
and other wetland species can continue to thrive and soar
from dawn to dusk.

Autumn

Falling

Y   E   L   L   O   W
             E
O   R   A   N   G   E
             V
    R   E   D
             S

turn brown
then become invisible
replenishing the earth.
In spring the blueprint of life presents
a budding new green presence
again.
What a colorful journey of the DNA life-force,
using energy and matter
to create a living community
of many different things.

Gratitude

When the eyes of the Red-eyed tree frog are closed,
the appearance is mostly green,
camouflaging with its lush habitat,
interspersed with blooming tropical colors.
Suddenly, opened bright red eyes startle its prey
into giveaway movements.
Sticky orange-red toes assist the climb
to a safe wherever.
Thank you Costa Rica for protecting
this forest ecosystem
where biodiversity thrives

Out of a Leathery Egg

Using a temporary egg tooth, the hatchling emerges.
The waterways are not what they used to be.
Fish, frogs, alligators, crocodiles and
other aquatic organisms
are exposed to life-changing chemicals in the water.
What happens then?
Back in the day when DDT ruled,
the weed killer streamed into waterways
and caused feminization of the male.
Now the new herbicides mimic estrogen
slowing down male development.
Both testes and ovaries develop.
There is concern that the rising rate of undescended
male sex organs, low sperm count and
birth defects in humans
in other parts of the world
might be showing the same effects
of these new herbicides.

Forethought

The Theodore Roosevelt National Park provides quiet spaces for nature seekers.
There are grassy plains for galloping wild horses, bison, elk, prairie dogs, and
badgers;
sandy and rocky landscapes for bighorn sheep and coyotes;
and mountains and forests for mule deer and many species of birds.
However, the outskirts of these communities are changing
due to a long line of 18-wheelers,
endless pumpjack activity,
and noisy construction.
Fracking, injecting chemicals, millions of gallons of water and sand
under high pressure, brings the underground oil
to the surface.
As a result, the levels of polluted water, toxic air, and radioactive wastes have
increased.
Good news! There are those who have proposed a limit
to the development en route to this place
with many different landscapes
and living species.
Then honor to our 26th president can be restored once again.
But
Fracking is occurring all over the U.S.,
even in earthquake areas.
Observation of a correlation is a good idea.
The human population is steadily increasing.
Enough fresh water for all is essential.

Crater Lake

Still, serene water reflects blue light that enchants.
Created by an erupted volcano,
the collapsed mountain then filled with melted snow and rain.
This wondrous blue caldera provides a retreat
from the noise and bustle
of crowded cities and routine busyness.
Your children's children deserve to see and be a part of
beautiful wild places, and clean resources.
Preserving the beauty and tranquility of our natural treasures
require responsibility.
How are you being responsible?
Are you
staying on designated trails?
refraining from dropping trash?
starting fires only when and where legal?
dousing fires completely?
returning too small fish back to the waterway?
gifting $$?
sounding the alarm to concerned citizens?
replanting native species?
Our parks are our unspoiled treasures.

Jacquelyn

Monarch Butterflies

Logging is removing trees
to which the Monarch returns after migration.
The overzealous use of herbicides
for unlabeled genetically modified foods
is also contributing to the decline of milkweed plants.
The hatched offspring must consume milkweed.
Plant milkweed,
milkweed,
and more milkweed
everywhere it is appropriate
Then migration of these polka-dotted
winged beauties
will thrive again
in healthy ecosystems
with less
toxic herbicides.

One Life

Interconnected in a dance
of light-energy
and matter,
elements combined,
exchanged,
recombined,
and spiraled into
a labyrinth .
Every action,
reaction,
interaction
and transaction
was an opportunity for change.
Connected to the same Source,
our choices can lead
to a harmony
of health and well-being
for Earth and its inhabitants.

Synchrony

Under cover of darkness, horseshoe crabs
crawl ashore with the high tide into Delaware Bay.
Suitable places beckon
the laying of eggs,
answering the call of perpetuation.
The next day these super-rich green eggs fuel the shorebirds
whose flight originated from Tierra del Fuego
on their way to the Arctic
to answer their own call.
Synchrony of this relationship depends upon –
steady ocean temperatures,
leak-proof ocean vessels,
conscientious research,
and a healthy balanced atmosphere.
Caring for the Earth is caring for our own survival!

Echoes of Silent Spring

The air is empty
of the flight of butterflies, bees, owls, bats, or birds.
Habitats are polluted.
Spring did not arrive.
The new biocides, neonics, killed the pollinators directly.
These weed killers were also absorbed by some plants
making them toxic to nectar sippers
and other herbivores.
So there is little food
and few flowers.
Life is crying out loud.
Let us listen,
make better choices,
and not let this happen.
Then spring will be filled with flying colors, fragrance,
and a chorus of songs, clicks, croaks, and calls.

Emerging

There is
an EMERGING consciousness of
collaboration,
compassion, and sustainability.
Let it be manifested
as it travels from New Zealand
westward all around the world.
Join together to celebrate the evolution.
One heartbeat

A Tribute to Birth Day
December 22, 2012

Acknowledgments

Thank you for your inspiration:

Natural Wildlife Federation
The Nature Conservancy
National Parks Conservation Association
The Wilderness Society
The Mouth and Foot Painting Artists
Science of Mind Magazine
National Geographic
Los Angeles Times
Living in the Environment / Eleventh Edition / G. Tyler Miller, Jr.
Environmental Science: A Global Concern / Cunningham & Saigo
Environment: The Science Behind the Stories / Withgott & Brennan
Mr. Hughes
Family and Friends

The Maya Taylor Scholarship

Together in your name, we celebrate the joy you brought to our lives, and are still bringing.

A scholarship from the sale of the framed artwork will be given to a graduating senior to honor a very sweet soul.

January 5, 1982 – February 15, 2004

Thank you for such a loving spirit!